ISBN 0 85079 141 3

AN EXPRESS BOOKS PUBLICATION

Printed by Eyre & Spottiswoode, Cosham, Hants. & co-ordinated by Roeder Print Services Ltd.

THE ADVENTURES OF LEGIONNAIRE
BEAU PEEP
FROM THE DAILY STAR AND SUNDAY EXPRESS MAGAZINE

YOU KNOW, DENNIS, SOME OF THESE STARS AREN'T REALLY THERE!

NO!

YES, THEY DISAPPEARED YEARS AGO BUT THE LIGHT STILL REACHES US.

SO ALTHOUGH WE SEE THEM ALL THE TIME, THERE'S ACTUALLY NOTHING BEHIND THE SPARKLE.

SORT OF COSMIC POLITICIANS.

LOOK WHAT I FOUND, BEAU.

IT LOOKS REALLY OLD. WHAT IS IT?

"AND THERE, 12 PACES EAST YOU WILL FIND THE HIDDEN GOLD."

IT'S A TR-TR-TRE-TREAS—

TRY TO OPEN YOUR FINGERS, BEAU.

DENNIS, WE'RE RICH!

IT'S A TREASURE MAP! IT SHOWS WHERE HIDDEN GOLD IS BURIED.

WE HAVE TO PREPARE OURSELVES FOR THE POSSIBILITY IT MAY BE A FAKE.

YOU'RE RIGHT.

I'M GOING TO HAVE TWO YACHTS WITH ALL-WOMEN CREWS!

I'LL HAVE TEN!

WE SHOULD BE VERY NEAR THE TREASURE NOW, DENNIS!

I'VE HIT SOMETHING!

IT'S BLACK, ABOUT A FOOT LONG AND COVERED WITH BLOOD!

ALL I'M SAYING IS, I WOULDN'T HAVE LAUGHED IF YOU'D DONE IT.

I STILL CAN'T BELIEVE HOW LUCKY YOU WERE FINDING THAT TREASURE MAP, DENNIS!

I KNOW! I JUST OPENED THE COMIC AND THERE IT WAS!

DENNIS, ARE YOU TELLING ME THIS MAP CAME FREE IN A COMIC?

YUP!

CHARGE FIVE — YOU THEN TOOK THE SPADE AND ATTEMPTED SOMETHING PHYSICALLY IMPOSSIBLE....

RIGHT, LADS, I'VE BEEN MADE AN ACTING CORPORAL...

1000

...BUT THERE WILL BE NO HEAVY-HANDED STUFF FROM ME.

IT MAY BE PROMOTION, BUT AFTER ALL, I'M STILL ONE OF THE BOYS.

EXCUSE ME, BEAU.

THAT'S 'CORPORAL' TO YOU, SONNY— SEVEN DAYS BREAD AND WATER!

LET'S GET ONE THING STRAIGHT, PIERRE— I'M THE ONE WHO'S BEEN MADE CORPORAL.

SO WHEN I SAY "DIG A FOX-HOLE" YOU DO IT!

WHACK!

1001

I TAKE YOUR POINT— A GOOD OFFICER SHOULD LEAD BY EXAMPLE!

MEN, THE SERGEANT WILL BE BACK TODAY AND MY STINT AS CORPORAL WILL BE OVER.

1002

I THINK WE CAN SAFELY TELL HIM I WAS HARD BUT FAIR...

...AND THAT DISCIPLINE REMAINED THROUGHOUT HIS ABSENCE.

HOLD ON, PIERRE— I HAVEN'T FINISHED YOUR SOCKS.

THIS IS A VERY EXCLUSIVE NEW CLUB, DENNIS.

CLUB DE FRANCE

1003

IT IS REPUTED TO HAVE CHARM, CLASS AND ELEGANCE.

CLUB DE

IN SHORT, A MAGNIFICENT PLACE.

WHAT ARE YOU TRYING TO SAY, BEAU?

NO BURPING.

SIR, I REALISE YOU'VE BEEN UNDER A BIT OF PRESSURE LATELY.

SOME OF YOUR ORDERS HAVE BEEN A BIT...ER... UNORTHODOX.

1014

AM I TO TAKE IT YOU'RE REFUSING A COMMAND, SERGEANT?

NO SIR!

THEN DRAW A FACE ON MY NOSE!

LINE THE MEN UP, SERGEANT. I'LL TAKE THEM FOR DRILL MYSELF.

YES, SIR.

THANK GOODNESS! I THINK THE COLONEL'S PULLED HIMSELF TOGETHER AGAIN.

1015

RIGHT, MEN, WHEN I GIVE THE WORD I WANT YOU TO START MARCHING.

BUT ONLY IF I SAY "SIMON SAYS" FIRST!

SARGE, CAN I HAVE A WORD?

WHAT CAN WE DO ABOUT THE COLONEL? HIS ORDERS GET DAFTER EVERY DAY!

IT'S ONLY TEMPORARY, PEEP. HE'LL BE BACK TO HIS OLD SELF IN NO TIME.

MEANWHILE, CARRY ON PAINTING THE SENTRY.

1016

WITH RESPECT, SIR, I THINK YOU SHOULD TAKE SOME LEAVE.

LEAVE!? I DON'T LIKE WHAT YOU'RE INSINUATING, SERGEANT!

THERE'S NOTHING WRONG WITH ME! BESIDES, I COULDN'T POSSIBLY GO ON LEAVE JUST NOW!

1017

I'VE ORGANISED A JOAN OF ARC LOOKALIKE CONTEST FOR TOMORROW!

WHAT A BEAUTIFUL NIGHT!

IT REMINDS ME OF THE NIGHT DORIS AND I WALKED HAND IN HAND ALONG THE BEACH.

1018

SHE WAS WEARING THAT LONG, WHITE DRESS OF HERS.

THAT POLICEMAN THOUGHT I WAS TOWING AN ICE-CREAM VAN.

I'VE BEEN THINKING OF MY DORIS A LOT LATELY.

1019

ONE DAY, I GOT HER A LITTLE PRESENT AND, THE ROMANTIC FOOL I AM, I HID IT IN HER GARDEN.

WHAT HAPPENED?

THE POSTMAN STOOD ON IT— DAMN NEAR BLEW HIS LEG OFF.

THE TIMES I HAD TO WAIT FOR MY DORIS TO PUT ON HER MAKE-UP!

1020

D'YOU KNOW, ONE TIME SHE WAS THREE HOURS AT IT!

TURNS OUT, THE HANDLE HAD SNAPPED OFF HER TROWEL.

I WROTE DORIS A COUPLE OF WEEKS BACK.

1021

I TOLD HER I'D BE THINKING OF HER AT FIVE O'CLOCK TODAY AND, IF SHE DID THE SAME, PERHAPS OUR MINDS COULD MEET.

THAT'S LOVELY, BEAU. I KNEW YOU REALLY LIKED HER

WELL, IT'S NEARLY FIVE. I MUST GO AND CLEAN OUT THE CAMELS.

ALL THAT'S NEEDED TO MAKE THIS TASTE DELICIOUS IS A DROP OF SHERRY.

GLOOP! GLOOP!

1032

CRASH!

IT'S A GIFT YOU'VE GOT, LAD, A GIFT!

I THINK I'LL PUT SHERRY TRIFLE ON THE MENU TODAY.

WITH SHERRY SOUP TO START FOLLOWED BY LAMB CHOPS IN SHERRY.

GLOOP! GLOOP!

1033

BEST DAMN BREAKFAST I'VE EVER MADE.

Dear Diary, today I am filled with pride!!

Why? Well, let me tell you!

While on patrol, we came under heavy fire.

And guess who hardly cried at all!

1044

Dear Diary, I am on patrol. All is quiet.

How long can this eerie silence last?

KL-UNK!

Only seconds! Bells are ringing, Birds are singing...

1045

SNAP!

VERY GOOD, DENNIS. YOU HAVE EXCEPTIONAL REFLEXES.

BUT ALLOW ME TO EXPLAIN THE RULES OF 'WHIST' AGAIN.

OH-OH, DENNIS MUST HAVE A DIFFICULT HAND TO ADD UP.

MUTTER!

HIS LITTLE BRAIN IS NOW AT MAXIMUM OUTPUT.

MUTTER!

WHAT TIME IS IT, DENNIS?

OVERLOAD.

CLUNK!

I'VE GOT A SORE LEG.

1060

IT'S NOT *VERY* SORE BUT IT'S *QUITE* SORE.

I'M DYING FOR THE TOILET BUT DARE I RISK MISSING THIS CLIFF-HANGER?

WELL, THANK YOU ONCE AGAIN, DENNIS!

BAR

YOU SEEM TO TAKE GREAT DELIGHT IN EMBARRASSING ME!

SO IT'S WRONG TO TELL A GIRL SHE'S GOT NICE TEETH!

YES, WHEN THEY'RE IN A GLASS!

1061

THE TROUBLE IS HE'S GOT NO SENSE OF HUMOUR.

1054

I DON'T THINK ANYTHING MAKES HIM LAUGH.

GUFFAW! HAW-HAW!

THAT OLD WOMAN JUST FELL OVER A ROCK!

WHY DON'T YOU EVER TELL JOKES, PIERRE—DON'T YOU KNOW ANY?

1055

ALL RIGHT, PEEP— I'LL TELL YOU A JOKE.

THE NEXT TIME I PUNCH YOU, YOU'LL STILL BE STANDING. HAW! HAW! THAT'S A REAL JOKE!

AND TO THINK PEOPLE SAY YOU'VE GOT NO SENSE OF HUMOUR!

GUESS WHAT, DENNIS! I'VE BEEN SUGGESTED FOR INTELLIGENCE WORK!

OH, YEAH? WHAT ABOUT ME?

DENNIS, IT DEPENDS ON LOTS OF THINGS— LENGTH OF SERVICE, BASIC SKILLS, ADAPTABILITY.

1072

BESIDES, YOU'RE STUPID.

I DON'T SEE WHY YOU'RE GOING TO DO INTELLIGENCE WORK AND I'M NOT!

WHY DON'T YOU ASK THE SERGEANT?

I WILL!

AND HE'D BETTER HAVE A GOOD REASON!

THAT DOOR OPENS OUTWARDS, DENNIS.

1073

COME.

SGT. BIDET

KNOCK! KNOCK!

1014

WHY CAN'T I DO INTELLIGENCE WORK?

ARE YOU CAPABLE OF LONG HOURS OF INTENSE CONCENTRATION?

SORRY, WHAT WAS THAT? I WAS MILES AWAY!

I'M FED UP CLEANING THE TOILETS! I WANT TO DO INTELLIGENCE WORK!

ALL RIGHT, I'LL TEST YOU. HOW WOULD YOU SET ABOUT DECIPHERING CAPTURED CODES?

1075

HAVE YOU SEEN MY MOP?

SOME PEOPLE THOUGHT I WAS GOING CRAZY BUT YOU DIDN'T, DID YOU, PEEP?

ER...NO, SIR!

THAT'S WHY I'M GOING TO PROMOTE YOU!

1078

TO...TO CORPORAL, SIR?

HIGHER!

KING OF THE JUMBLIES!

PEEP, I'D LIKE YOU TO DO SOMETHING FOR ME.

SIR?

SAY "YIP-YIP-YAHOO."

1079

"YIP-YIP YAHOO," SIR?

YOU'RE MY KINDA GUY, PEEP!

NOW, SIR, TWO VEAL CUTLETS WITH HOUSE SALADS.

1084

THIS LOOKS DELICIOUS—AND WHAT SUPERB SERVICE!

SHALL I TOSS YOUR SALAD, SIR?

NO, JUST HAND IT TO ME.

THIS IS A GREAT PUDDING! HOI! WAITER!

I'M IN THE TRADE, TOO, AND I WAS WONDERING IF YOU'D ASK THE CHEF FOR THIS PUDDING RECIPE.

1085

I'M AFRAID THE CHEF NEVER GIVES OUT HIS RECIPES BUT I'LL PASS ON ANY MESSAGE YOU'D LIKE TO SEND.

A CONCISE, LITTLE MESSAGE, EGON.

WELL, I LEARNED NOTHING THERE. THE FOOD'S RUBBISH.

AND DID YOU SEE THAT SLUG IN MY SALAD?

1086

YES, I MUST ADMIT THAT WAS DISGRACEFUL.

I'LL SAY! THERE WAS HARDLY A MOUTHFUL IN IT!

IT'S MY TRIBE! I HAVEN'T SEEN THEM FOR AGES.

1087

THEY'VE PROBABLY FORGOTTEN MY BANISHMENT AND WILL WELCOME ME WITH OPEN ARMS!

FRIENDS, BROTHERS, I HAVE RETURNED! LET US CELEBRATE!

NOTHING FANCY— A CUP OF TEA WOULD DO FINE!

I'M GLAD I'M BANISHED! I DON'T WANT TO COME BACK TO THE TRIBE!

1090

BECAUSE I'M A LONER! A RENEGADE! A FEARSOME WARRIOR WHO SHUNS THE COMPANY OF OTHERS!

THUMP!

I REVEL IN THE SOLITUDE OF THE BURNING SANDS!

THOUGH I TEND TO GET A TEENY BIT NERVOUS WHEN IT'S DARK.

WELL, I'M STILL ON MY OWN.

1091

A SOLITARY FIGURE DOOMED TO WANDER FOREVER WITHOUT COMPANIONSHIP.

STILL, IT SAVES HAVING TO PASS ROUND MY JELLY-BABIES.

RUSTLE!

WHAT ARE YOU DOING, DENNIS?

I'M MAKING A MATCHSTICK MODEL.

IT'S GOING TO BE THE LEANING TOWER OF PARIS.

I WON'T SAY ANYTHING, I'LL ASSUME THAT WAS A SLIP OF THE TONGUE.

YOU KNOW THE ONE— IT'S GOT A CLOCK CALLED BEN NEVIS IN IT.

HERE COMES PEEP! NOW'S MY CHANCE TO NIP OUT AND SLAUGHTER HIM!

I'LL LET HIM GO, IT'S BETTER TO BE COMPASSIONATE AND FORGIVING.

ALSO, I'VE GOT MY PINKY STUCK BETWEEN THESE ROCKS.

AND DON'T COME BACK!

BOOT!

CAN I HAVE MY WOODEN CAMEL? I SPENT HOURS MAKING THAT!

YOU HID IN THAT CAMEL SO YOU COULD SNEAK OUT AND KILL US. HOW COULD YOU EXPECT US TO GIVE IT BACK!

1191

BUT MY JELLY-BABIES ARE IN IT!

THERE'S NOTHING ECCENTRIC ABOUT ME, PEEP.

PEOPLE TEND TO CONFUSE MADNESS WITH GENIUS.

THAT'S BEEN THE CURSE OF GREAT MILITARY TACTICIANS LIKE MYSELF FOR CENTURIES.

ANYWAY, AS I WAS SAYING, WE'LL ADVANCE ON THE ENEMY DRESSED AS CAULIFLOWERS.

WHAT MAKES SOMEONE WRITE A POEM, BEAU?

A GOOD QUESTION, DENNIS, IT'S USUALLY SOMETHING THAT STIRS AN EMOTION IN THEM.

SOMETHING WHICH THEY FEEL VERY DEEPLY ABOUT.

IN YOUR CASE, PYJAMAS WITH LITTLE TRAINS ON THEM.

1194

"I WANDERED LONELY AS A CLOUD..."

THAT'S STUPID.

STUPID IS IT! OH, SORRY, MR. WORDSWORTH! DENNIS THINKS YOU'RE STUPID!

RIP!

MIGHT AS WELL GET RID OF SHELLEY AND KEATS AS WELL! THEY'RE STUPID TOO!

I MEANT THE WAY YOUR MOUSTACHE WIGGLES WHEN YOU READ.

1195

AND YOU'LL STAY THERE UNTIL YOU LEARN TO OBEY AN ORDER!

LEFT ALONE UNDER A BAKING SUN — IT'S INHUMAN!

SE38

IT'S DENNIS! AT LAST A BIT OF COMPASSION FROM A COMRADE!

COULD YOU KEEP YOUR HEAD STILL WHILE I DO THIS TOAST?

EVENING, PEEP.

EVENING, SIR.

I'M HERE TO TELL YOU TO KEEP YOUR EYES OPEN TONIGHT.

SE36

DO YOU KNOW WHY, PEEP?

ER...NO, SIR.

WELL, IF YOU DON'T, I'M PRETTY SURE YOU'LL FALL OFF THE WALL.

I WAS REALLY SPOILING FOR A FIGHT! WE SHOULD HAVE ATTACKED THAT LOT.

PIERRE, SURELY THERE'S SOME OTHER WAY YOU CAN GET RID OF ALL THAT PENT-UP AGGRESSION?

WHACK!

THAT'S THE BIT THAT GETS ME— THE SPLIT SECOND BETWEEN THE STUPID QUESTION AND THE LIGHTS GOING OUT.

1096

I'LL TAKE OVER, DENNIS—ANYTHING TO REPORT?

YES, THERE IS. IT WAS REALLY WIERD.

1097

I KEPT HEARING STRANGE NOISES AND I COULD SEE A SORT OF PIG-LIKE...

IT'S YOUR DORIS AGAIN, ISN'T IT?

CLUNK!

IT'S THE WAITING I HATE!

KNOWING THAT SOMEWHERE OUT THERE MY DORIS IS LURKING.

WHY DOESN'T SHE JUST COME UP TO THE FORT?

IT'S DAYLIGHT— SHE KNOWS I COULD PICK HER OFF FROM HERE.

1098

COOEE! BEAU, IT'S ME! I LOVE YOU!

GO AWAY, DORIS!

1099

BUT, BEAU, I'VE COME ALL THIS WAY JUST TO SEE YOU!

WELL, AT LEAST, TURN ROUND—YOU'RE FRIGHTENING THE CAMELS.

SERGEANT, YOU'VE GOT TO HELP ME!

IT'S MY DORIS— SHE'S OUTSIDE THE GATE!

WHAT CAN I DO?

I DON'T WANT TO SEE HER BUT I DON'T WANT TO HURT HER FEELINGS.

SO?

1100

PERMISSION TO SHOOT HER, SIR?

YOUR DORIS HAS LEFT.

SHE HAS?

1101

SHE SAID SHE UNDERSTOOD THAT YOU COULDN'T SEE HER AND SHE'D COME BACK SOON.

THEN SHE SAID SHE'D JUST WALK OFF INTO THE SETTING SUN.

I THOUGHT IT WAS GETTING DARK—IT'S LIKE AN ECLIPSE.

RIGHT, THIS LOOKS ABOUT PERFECT.

1108

NOW I'LL WORK OUT THE TERMS FOR THEIR SURRENDER.

" I WILL BLAST YOUR FORT TO BITS UNLESS YOU HAND OVER YOUR JELLY-BABIES."

MY GOD, IF THAT DOESN'T GET THE WHITE FLAG RUNNING UP THE POLE, NOTHING WILL!

ALL RIGHT YOU LOT— SURRENDER!

1109

YOU'VE ASKED FOR IT! I'M GOING TO OPEN FIRE!

BOOM! WHEEÉ!

I'M RATHER HOPING THEY DON'T NOTICE I'VE GOT NO AMMUNITION.

WHAT ARE YOU DOING, BEAU?

A CRYPTIC CROSSWORD.

HERE IT COMES— HE'S GOING TO PRETEND HE KNOWS WHAT A CRYPTIC CROSSWORD IS.

I'VE DONE LOTS OF THEM.

1112

CAN I COLOUR IN THE WHITE BITS?

GO ON, READ ME A CROSSWORD CLUE—I BET I CAN DO IT!

1113

ALL RIGHT, DENNIS— "LANCE BROKEN BUT SPOTLESS." FIVE LETTERS.

WELL, WHAT'S THE ANSWER?

WAS THAT THE CLUE? I THOUGHT THAT YOU'D JUST GONE DAFT.

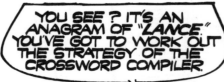

PEEP'S STILL MISSING.

1/20

I ONLY HOPE ONE OF THE PATROLS I SENT OUT FINDS HIM.

ONE GOOD THING ABOUT PEEP — HE WON'T CRACK UNDER PRESSURE.

HERE WE GO GATHERING NUTS IN MAY, NUTS IN MAY...

LOOK — IT'S BEAU! WE'VE FOUND HIM!

1/21

BEAU, IT'S GREAT TO SEE YOU! AND YOU'RE OKAY?

FINE!

THE SARGE SAID YOU MIGHT BE AFFECTED BY THE SUN.

NOT ME!

OH, HOW STUPID OF ME! DENNIS, THIS IS DEREK — DEREK, MEET DENNIS.

WELL, IT'S BEEN NICE TALKING TO YOU BUT I'VE GOT TO GO NOW.

1126

CHARMING! I SPEND HALF AN HOUR UNDERWATER WAITING TO AMBUSH HIM...

...AND THEN, JUST AS I'M ABOUT TO KILL HIM, A CAMEL RUNS ME OVER...

...AND NOW YOU WON'T EVEN STOP FOR A CHAT!

PEEP, THERE'S SOMETHING I WANT YOU TO DO FOR ME.

IT'S VERY DIFFICULT AND I'M NOT SURE IT CAN BE DONE.

1127

BUT, BY HEAVENS, I KNOW YOU'LL GIVE IT A GO!

CAN YOU TOUCH THE TIP OF YOUR NOSE WITH YOUR TONGUE?

I'M READING A MARVELLOUS BOOK, DENNIS.

IT'S ALL ABOUT FAMOUS HISTORICAL PERSONALITIES LIKE ABRAHAM LINCOLN.

1/32

HE WAS SHOT IN A THEATRE, YOU KNOW.

I'VE SEEN A FEW ACTS LIKE THAT MYSELF.

IT'S WONDERFUL TO READ ABOUT HISTORY, DENNIS.

1/33

IT'S AS THOUGH YOU'RE ACTUALLY LIVING IN THE TIMES!

YOU CAN IMAGINE WHAT IT WAS LIKE TO STAND ON THE BRIDGE WITH NELSON.

YEAH, AN' WATCH THE TRAINS GO UNDERNEATH!

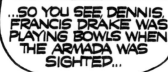

YOU KNOW WHAT I'M GOING TO DO, PIERRE? I'M GOING TO BUY YOU A DRINK...

...BECAUSE I THINK YOU COULD DO WITH ONE...

...AND BECAUSE YOU AND ME ARE BUDDIES!

NOT BECAUSE YOU'RE TWISTING MY FOOT!

1142

...AND THEN, YOU SEE, THE BALL BROKE LOOSE...

...I GOT THERE FIRST AHEAD OF THIS OTHER BLOKE...

1143

...SO I SMASHED HIM ONE, THEN JUMPED ON HIM BEFORE SETTING OFF WITH THE BALL.

GOOD GAME, TABLE TENNIS.

WHY IS IT ALWAYS ME?

EVERY TIME SOMETHING DANGEROUS COMES UP YOU PICK ME!

1152

PEEP THERE ARE CERTAIN MISSIONS WHICH ONLY THE BRAVEST AND THE BEST CAN HANDLE.

THEN THERE'S THIS SORT FOR COWARDY-CUSTARDS LIKE YOU.

IT'S NOT A VERY NICE THOUGHT, YOU KNOW, SERGEANT!

BEING SENT ON A MISSION KNOWING THAT YOU DON'T CARE IF I COME BACK OR NOT!

1153

YOU DON'T, DO YOU? YOU DON'T CARE IF I LIVE OR DIE!

PUT THAT BOOK DOWN AND ANSWER ME!

THERE MAY BE SOME ENEMY TRACKERS AROUND — I'LL TRY TO CONFUSE THEM.

1156

I'LL PUT MY LEFT BOOT ON MY RIGHT HAND AND MY RIGHT BOOT ON MY LEFT HAND...

...THEN I'LL SKIP BACKWARDS WITH A LIMP...

...AND KNOCK MYSELF OUT ON A PALM TREE.

WHATEVER HAPPENS, I MUSTN'T LET THEM FIND MY SECRET ENVELOPE!

IF THAT ENVELOPE FALLS INTO THEIR HANDS IT COULD BE DISASTROUS!

1157

LUCKILY, I'VE HIDDEN IT IN MY TUNIC!

TALK OR TORTURE?

I'VE GOT A LETTER FOR YOU!

PEOPLE DON'T REALISE WHAT A SENSITIVE SOUL I AM.

I DON'T KNOW WHAT I'LL DO IF I HEAR ONE MORE JOKE ABOUT MY COOKING.

1162

HELLO, EGON. HAVE YOU COME UP HERE TO THROW YOUR CAKES AT THE ENEMY?

ISN'T THAT EGON HOLDING BEAU OVER THE WALL BY THE ANKLES.

EGON! D-DON'T DO ANYTHING HASTY!

FOR EVERY JOKE YOU MADE ABOUT MY COOKING, YOU'RE GOING TO SUFFER AN INDESCRIBABLE HORROR.

1163

LOOK, NO HANDS!

AAARGH!

THAT WAS FOR THE LITTLE JOKE ABOUT MY JAM ROLY-POLY.

THE COLONEL WANTS US TO LOOK AFTER THIS LOBSTER. WHAT CAN WE DO?

MAYBE I COULD TEACH IT TO FETCH STICKS!

1174

DENNIS, WE'RE TALKING ABOUT A DUMB CREATURE WHOSE HOBBY IS BLOWING BUBBLES.

COME TO THAT, THE LOBSTER'S NONE TOO BRIGHT EITHER.

I WANT YOU TO THINK UP A GOOD NAME FOR OUR NEW MASCOT THE LOBSTER.

SOMETHING BRAVE AND COURAGEOUS, SOMETHING STEEPED IN FIGHTING TRADITION!

A NAME WHICH CONJURES VISIONS OF A BATTLE-HARDENED VETERAN!

1175

I'VE BROUGHT LUCY HER TEA.

DENNIS, I CAN'T WRITE THIS.

WHY NOT?

YOU WANT RUDOLPH TO GO ON STRIKE IF SANTA DOESN'T GIVE YOU A PRESENT.

YES.

WELL, I SUPPOSE THAT PART'S NOT TOO BAD.

IT'S THIS BIT ABOUT GETTING THE WHOLE HERD TO STAMPEDE HIS TOY SHOP.

DENNIS, THIS IS STUPID!

RIP!

I AM NOT WRITING TO SANTA, RUDOLPH OR ANY OTHER REINDEER!

I'M SORRY, BEAU. YOU'RE RIGHT — IT IS STUPID.

I'LL SHOUT IT UP THE CHIMNEY!

Panel 1: DIDN'T YOU HAVE ANY FRIENDS AT SCHOOL, PIERRE?

Panel 2: I USED TO PLAY DARTS WITH ONE BLOKE.

1184

Panel 4: THAT SMILE SUGGESTS HIS PARTNER HAD A POINTED HEAD.

Panel 5: DESPITE THE TOUGH EXTERIOR, PIERRE IS A VERY LONELY MAN.

Panel 6: I'M SURE ALL HIS VIOLENCE STEMS FROM A LACK OF FRIENDS.

Panel 7: IT'S UP TO THE REST OF US TO BREAK DOWN THE BARRIER, TO SHOW AN INTEREST IN HIM.

1185

Panel 8: HOW MANY EARS DO YOU HAVE IN YOUR COLLECTION NOW, PIERRE?

For further adventures of Legionnaire Beau Peep see the

ALL THIS STUFF ABOUT DREAMS AND CARDS IS NONSENSE!

I MEAN, HALF THE TIME I DREAM ABOUT NOTHING!

DOES THAT MEAN *I'M* A NOTHING?

I ASK SOME GREAT QUESTIONS.

/201/

WILL IT NEVER CEASE BEATING DOWN?

DAMN THAT MERCILESS SUN!

WHY?

IT'S FADED MY NEW BLUE HANKY.

IT'S WONDERFUL ISN'T IT?

MEN MARCHING IN AND OUT OF THE GATES, HORSES, CANNONS AND FLAGS.

1204

THANK GOODNESS HE'S GOT OVER ALL THAT SANTA CLAUS NONSENSE!

THAT'S WHAT'S IN THE TOY FORT SANTA'S BRINGING ME!

SORRY ABOUT GOING ON ABOUT SANTA SO MUCH.

1205

STUPID KID'S STUFF! I DON'T BELIEVE IN HIM ANYWAY!

BRRR! MY LEFT FOOT IS COLD!

NO, DENNIS.

PLEASE, PLEASE LEND ME YOUR LONG SOCK!